Easy Vegetable Growing

Contents

Spade Work

To grow vegetables successfully a gardener needs to understand his soil. Soil varies widely in its texture—even in the same garden or allotment there can be variations. Soils may be described as light, medium or heavy. When gardeners talk of 'a good loam' they are describing a good, average soil.

A light soil is one where sand particles predominate. Light soils are easy to work but dry out quickly and need plenty of humus. A medium loam is one where the sand and clay particles are in roughly equal proportions. This type of soil will grow almost anything and blessed is the gardener who has it ! A heavy soil is one which has a preponderance of clay. Clay soils are more difficult to work but do not dry out quickly. The best time to break down a clay soil is when the soil is beginning to dry out after reasonable rainfall. Do not trample a clay soil when it is wet or it will set like concrete.

'Topsoil' is the upper, fertile layer of soil ; 'subsoil' is the layer beneath the topsoil and is usually low in fertility. The fertility of subsoils can be increased by double-digging, manuring and liming, but unless you are growing vegetables for exhibition, this deep cultivation is not necessary. It is enough to work the soil to the depth of the spade.

Single digging is the turning over of the soil to a spade's depth. This should be done in autumn or winter, leaving the clods of earth where they fall. Frosts, which cause contraction and expansion of the soil, will break it down for spring sowings.

Clay soils can be improved by winter ridging. To make a ridge, mark out a

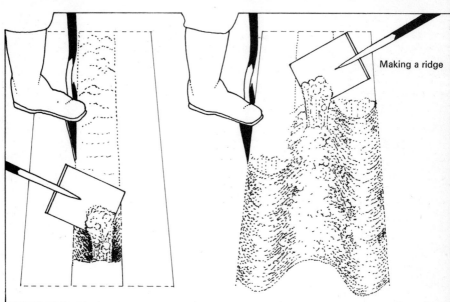

Making a ridge

strip three spadefuls wide. Dig the centre spit (spadeful) over itself, then turn the outer spits over the centre one. This exposes a larger area of soil to the winter weather. In the spring rake the ridges down again.

Before any vegetables are sown, measure up the plot and then make out a crop plan to fit the available space. Keep a copy of this list for future reference. Most vegetables benefit from a change of soil, and it will prevent the build-up of pests and diseases. This is known as crop rotation. A simple form of a three-year crop rotation, dividing the plot into three parts, is given here:

	Part A	Part B	Part C
1st yr	Greens	Potatoes	Other crops
2nd yr	Potatoes	Other crops	Greens
3rd yr	Other crops	Greens	Potatoes

Exceptions to this rule of crop rotation are asparagus and rhubarb which, once planted, should remain there to mature for many years. These are often sited across one end of the plot. As a vegetable plot has to be tailored to the needs of the individual family, each gardener must work out his own system of crop rotation.

Consideration should also be given to the possible limitations of the plot. In a shallow soil, for example, it would be pointless to sow long beetroot, long carrots, or the largest parsnips. Globe beetroot, shorthorn carrots and half-long parsnips would be the varieties to choose. Similarly, if the plot is an exposed one, the tall broad beans and Brussels sprouts may suffer wind damage. In this case, the half-tall varieties of sprouts and the dwarf broad beans would be a better choice.

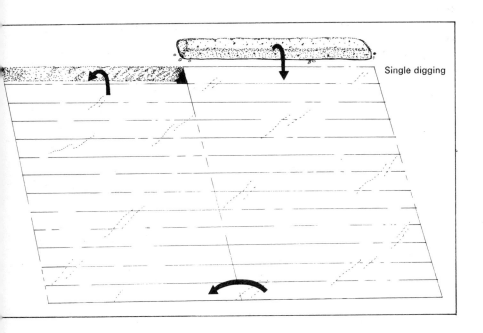

Single digging

Soil Fertility

The importance of building up and maintaining the fertility of the vegetable plot can never be stressed too much. In general, vegetables need a more fertile soil than flowers and some, such as onions and cauliflowers, are gross feeders and will not do their best in a poor soil.

Plants feed on the mineral salts in the soil and take them in by means of tiny root hairs. The essential plant foods are nitrogen, phosphates and potash. Nitrogen is necessary for growth and leaf formation ; phosphates increase root growth and assist ripening, and potash improves the general health and vigour of the plant by promoting root activity. There are other chemicals which are needed only in minute quantities and which are known as 'trace elements'. Iron and boron are two of these. Trace elements are usually present in any good garden soil and do not normally require special attention.

There are two ways of supplying the essential plant foods to the soil. One is by the application of bulky organic manures, such as farmyard and stable manures, which are dug into the soil during autumn and winter. Once in the soil, they are attacked by soil bacteria which break up the vegetable wastes and reduce them to a brown, friable medium called humus. Humus improves the soil structure, releases plant foods slowly, and acts like a sponge to retain moisture.

The other method is to use inorganic manures (fertilizers). These are man-made compounds of mineral salts, scientifically produced and offered in powdered or granular form. They are generally used as 'top dressings' (ie they are sprinkled around the plants and hoed in). Rain washes them down to the roots of the plants. They act quickly but need to be used with care.

The drawback of using fertilizers is that they neither make humus nor improve the soil structure. Used continuously in a soil that is short of humus they tend to leave the soil sticky and intractable. The essential point to keep in mind is that while fertilizers can supplement organic manuring, they cannot replace it.

To keep the soil fertile, some form of organic manuring is essential. Unfortunately, farmyard manure is becoming more difficult to obtain, so you may have to look round for other sources of supply. Horse manure from riding stables, spent mushroom compost, spent hops from breweries, deep litter from poultry houses, seaweed, and sewage are some alternatives. Many local authorities now process their sewage and offer it in an acceptable form.

Every gardener has a good source of humus-making material right on his doorstep. Any organic rubbish forked into a heap will rot down to make compost. Good compost is high on the list of organic manures and is quickly incorporated in the soil.

Kitchen waste, leaves of brassicas and lettuces, straw, green haulms (stems or stalks), weeds (but not the roots of perennial weeds), leaves and lawn mowings can all be used to make compost. The only items which need to be excluded are hardwood hedge-

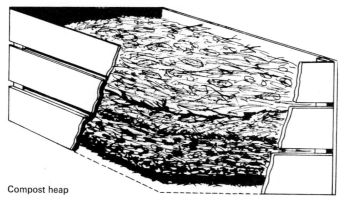

Compost heap

cuttings and green haulms suspected of carrying disease.

To make good compost, a bin of some kind is needed. Proprietary bins are available, but a simple container can be made quite easily by using strong wire netting nailed to corner posts. An alternative to this would be to nail boards to the corner posts. A little gap should then be left between the boards to admit air to the heap, and it would be an advantage if one end could be made detachable so that the contents could be shovelled out more easily. A bin about 122cm × 90cm (4ft × 3ft) is a useful size.

Build up the heap with 15cm (6in) layers of material, mixed for preference, and cover each layer with a sprinkling of a proprietary compost activator, or a dusting of hydrated lime. When the heap is 90–122cm (3–4ft) in height, finish it off with a cap of soil and then leave it to rot down. This process may be completed in as little as three months in spring and summer; a winter heap takes longer. Where small quantities of animal manures can be obtained, such as poultry or rabbit droppings, it is a good plan to use a layer of these between each layer of greenstuff.

Another method of making humus is by green manuring. This is the practice of growing a green crop especially for digging in, and rape or mustard are the plants most commonly used for this purpose. Ground which becomes vacant during the summer, and which is not needed again immediately, can be sown broadcast with rape or mustard. The plants should be dug in just as they are coming into flower.

Liquid manuring is another method of feeding plants. This should be applied when the soil is damp, at about fortnightly intervals. Proprietary liquid manures can be bought from garden centres or seedsmen. If an old tub is available, a supply can be made by putting a few forkfuls of manure in a hessian sack and suspending it in a tubful of water. Sheep manure is particularly good for this purpose. The 'brew' should be diluted until it is about the consistency and colour of weak tea. Keep the tub covered and make sure that children cannot get into it.

Another method of feeding plants can be effected through their leaves with a proprietary foliar feed, given through a sprayer or a watering-can. It is of special value for well foliated crops.

Basic Tools

The basic tools needed for the cultivation of a vegetable plot may be listed as follows : a spade, fork, rake, hoe, cultivator, dibber, trowel, garden-line and measuring-stick. Stainless steel tools are lighter to use and do not require cleaning but cost more.

Spades come in several sizes. One with a blade about 28cm (11in) long and 20cm (8in) wide is a good, average size.

The digging fork should have four square tines (prongs). There are also forks with flat tines, which are useful for lifting potatoes, as fewer tubers will slip through the prongs. It is not necessary to have both, and if a choice has to be made, the digging fork should be chosen, as this is a more general-purpose fork.

Many of the rakes offered in shops are more suitable for flower borders than the vegetable plot. Soil that is raked down too finely produces more weeds. It is worth looking for a strong rake with a head about 38cm (15in) wide, and teeth about 5cm (2in) apart.

There are several types of hoes. In order to use the draw hoe, it should be extended and then pulled through the soil towards the user ; a Dutch hoe has the reverse action, as the blade is pushed away from the user. A good Dutch hoe is a useful tool, especially if it is the modern kind with a two-edged, serrated blade, but the draw hoe has a wider scope as it can be used for earthing-up and drawing seed drills. (The corner of the hoe is used for this, close up against the garden-line.) The little onion hoe is also a good buy as it can be used close to the rows. This cuts down hand-weeding.

The cultivator is used for breaking down the soil in spring and also for aerating the soil between rows of plants. It is pulled through the soil towards the user who has to walk backwards. Some cultivators have three spoonlike prongs ; some have five, and there is a more elaborate one with prongs which can be adjusted or removed altogether.

The dibber and trowel perform similar functions. A dibber has a short handle and a pointed end with a steel tip. It comes into its own when making holes for brassicas and leeks. Some gardeners prefer to use a trowel, however, even for leeks, and for moving plants with a good soil ball the trowel is the better tool.

Money spent on a good garden-line is never wasted as a home-made line made from odd pieces of string is never satisfactory. But do take the line indoors when it is not in use—it will last twice as long.

A good measuring-stick can be made quite cheaply at home from a length of lath. A piece 90cm (36in) in length, marked off at 15cm (6in) intervals, is a handy size.

Good tools are worth looking after. Keeping them clean and rubbing them over with an oily rag, when they are not in use, doesn't take long, but prolongs their life and makes all the difference when you next use them.

You will need to add a watering-can or hose to the above list. An old bucket costs nothing and is always useful. A wheelbarrow has many uses and is a good investment.

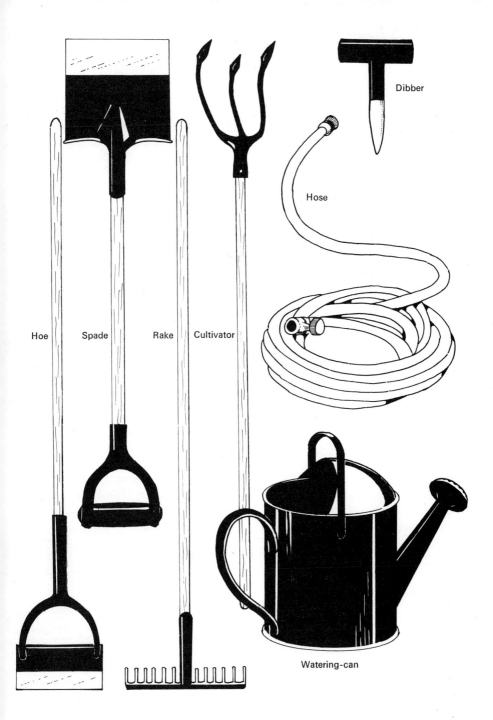

Dibber

Hose

Hoe   Spade   Rake   Cultivator

Watering-can

Asparagus

Although asparagus may be considered by some people to be a luxury vegetable rather than a basic one, its cultivation is not as difficult as many people suppose. The main disadvantage of growing asparagus is that it does take up quite a lot of room and will need to occupy that room permanently—a good asparagus bed can crop for twenty years, or more.

The plants can be raised from seeds which are sown in April in drills 2cm (1in) deep and 30cm(12in) apart. The seedlings should be thinned to stand 30cm (12in) apart. In their second season it will be possible to select the best plants for the permanent bed. This is the slowest method; it is more usual to buy two-year-old plants from seedsmen or nurserymen.

Asparagus plants are either male or female. The female plants bear berries; the males do not. It is generally accepted that male plants give a higher yield, but as male and female plants are produced in about equal numbers, some females usually have to be included to make up the required number.

Whether the plants are raised at home or bought in, no planting should be done until the site has been thoroughly prepared. It is worth doing the initial preparation well as there will not be another opportunity. All perennial weeds must be forked out and eliminated. Dig in as much compost or manure as you can spare so that the plants have a good start. In light or medium soils it is worth double-digging the chosen strip

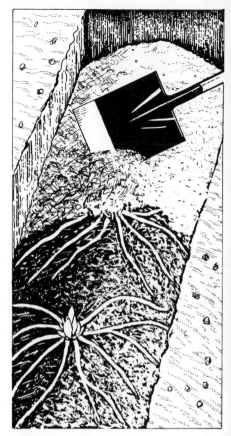

Planting asparagus

which sould be in a sunny, open position. On heavy soils, it is a good plan to make a raised bed with an extra 25–30cm (10–12in) of good topsoil. The site preparation should be completed by February so that the soil has time to settle before planting. A strip 2m (6ft) wide will take two rows 75cm (30in) apart.

To plant asparagus, take out a trench 30cm (12in) wide and 30cm (12in) deep. Put back enough soil in the trench to form a ridge 23cm (9in) high. Sit the plants on this ridge, with the spidery roots down each side of the

8

Cutting asparagus

middle of April to the middle of June. After this period sticks which appear should be allowed to grow on and form their feathery foliage. This builds up the crowns for the following season. Some twigs pushed in among the foliage, or string run from bamboo canes, will prevent the foliage from being blown down and broken off.

To maintain the bed in good condition, cut down the yellowing foliage each autumn and burn it; clear the bed of weeds, and then put on an inch or two of good compost. In April top dress the bed with a nitrogenous fertilizer, or agricultural salt, at about 70g per sq m (2oz per sq yd).

The main pest to look out for is the asparagus beetle which appears in July and August. This damages the plants by attacking the young shoots and foliage. Derris or BHC, sprayed or dusted over the bed, will usually control it.

Another trouble which may be encountered is asparagus rust. This fungus covers the stems and foliage with a reddish dust which is followed by black pustules on the next season's growth. Dusting with flowers of sulphur is a good safeguard. If good hygiene is observed by clearing away and burning the dying foliage in autumn, rust should not be a serious problem.

Recommended varieties
Connover's Colossal, the most popular variety
Martha Washington, a more recent introduction that shows some resistance to asparagus rust

ridge, and allow 45cm (18in) between the plants. The crown of each plant, when the trench is filled in, will then be about 8cm (3in) below the soil surface. An important point to remember is that the roots of asparagus should never be allowed to dry out. Keep them covered until planting takes place, then cover them again immediately.

Sticks should not be cut from the bed the first season after planting. In the second year take only one or two sticks from each plant. By the third year the bed will be well established. Cutting takes place from about the

Broad Beans

The bean family is one of the most useful to the vegetable gardener and the broad bean, although not as popular as the runner, is very tasty, especially when served with parsley sauce. It is not demanding in its soil requirements and any good garden soil should grow broad beans.

The best broad beans come from a sowing made in November. Unfortunately, the modern broad bean seems to have lost some of the hardiness of its ancestors and, in most districts, protection in the form of cloches is necessary in the winter months. The other sowing period is from February to April.

There are two types of broad bean, the tall and the dwarf. For some reason the dwarf broad bean has not yet achieved the popularity it deserves. It is especially valuable in gardens which suffer wind damage. The plants branch naturally to give several stems and they crop well.

The tall varieties can be divided into two groups : the longpods and the Windsors. The Windsors are a little shorter in the pod with slightly larger beans. Some people think that the Windsors have a better flavour.

There are two ways of sowing the tall beans. One method, if more than two rows are needed, is to sow them in drills 5cm (2in) deep, with 45cm (18in) between the rows and 20cm (8in) between the beans. The other, and the more usual method, is to sow a double row with a 25cm (10in) gap. To fill up possible spaces, always sow a few extra seeds at one end of the

Dwarf beans

rows. For the dwarf varieties allow 30cm (12in) between the seeds and 38cm (15in) between the rows.

It is advisable to stake the tall varieties. This can be done quite easily by pushing bamboo canes into the soil at intervals and then running stout string or garden wire from cane to cane. Plants at the ends of the rows are the most vulnerable. Tie these individually to the encircling string.

Tall beans

When the first pods have set and are forming, pinch out the growing tip of each plant. This turns the plant's energy into the production of pods and also prevents the blackfly from congregating in the soft tip, a favourite haunt.

Picking should begin when the seeds are about as big as a finger-nail. At this stage they are delicious. It is a mistake to leave them too long because once the pods are streaked with black, the seeds have begun to ripen and the skins toughen. Nowadays, as broad beans freeze well, there is no reason why any part of the crop should not be picked at its best.

Blackfly is the most serious menace to broad beans. However, if the plants are sprayed with derris or malathion at the first sign of this pest, or even earlier as a precautionary measure, no real harm should ensue.

Recommended varieties

Windsor : Green Windsor and White
    Windsor are the standard varieties
Longpod : Colossal, Bunyard's
    Exhibition. Aquadulce for autumn
    sowing
Dwarf : The Sutton

Blackfly

French and Haricot Beans

There are two types of French bean, the climbing and the dwarf ; of the two, the dwarf bean is more common. It is not as hardy as the broad bean and should not appear above ground while there is any likelihood of frost. This means that, except in milder areas, it should not be sown outdoors before the middle of May.

Although not quite as vigorous as the runner bean, the climbing French bean will still reach a height of 1.5m (5ft) and some form of staking is essential. Tall sticks of brushwood, and pea or bean netting are two methods. Where there is a trellis, or a wire fence of the chain-link type, the beans can be sown about 5cm (2in) deep and 15cm (6in) apart, about 23cm (9in) from the foot of the wire or trellis.

The dwarf varieties are grown in rows 60cm (24in) apart with 15–20cm (6–8in) between the beans. Another way of growing them, if only two rows are needed, is to sow them in a double row, with the two rows 30cm (12in) apart. This is a good method if you wish to use cloches. Sowing under cloches can take place in the second half of April.

French beans are not demanding in their soil requirements and a soil that was manured for a previous crop will be suitable. A sunny, open position is best for them. Their main enemy is slugs, but slug pellets, put down as soon as the plants are breaking through the soil, will give adequate protection.

Although dwarf beans are supposed not to need staking, it is a good plan

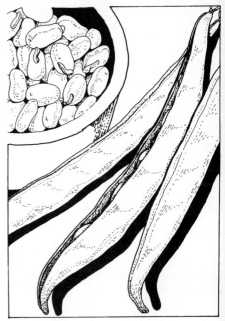

Haricot beans

to push in some twiggy sticks among them to keep them upright. If the plants fall over with the weight of the crop, some of the beans will be at soil level and may be attacked by slugs.

The pods of dwarf beans may be flat, like a smaller edition of the runner bean, or round like a pencil. Whatever form they take they should be gathered young and before the pods become lumpy with seeds. Pick the plants over two or three times each week. Cropping should continue for about six weeks. To prolong the season it is a good plan to make a second sowing in June.

Haricot beans are grown for the seeds, and the plants are left to form seeds from the beginning. There are certain varieties of dwarf beans which are suitable for this purpose, and their cultivation is the same as for dwarf beans.

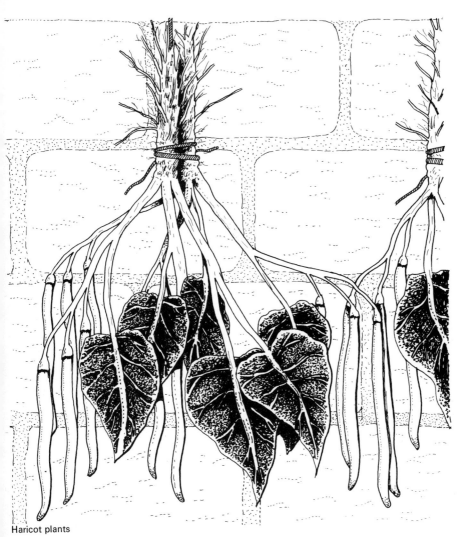

Haricot plants

When the seeds are ripe, the pods will be grey and dry. In a good summer they will often ripen on the plants. In cooler, showery weather, wait until the plants have turned yellow (about late September) then pull them up, tie them in bundles and hang them on a sunny wall to dry. The beans, when shelled out, can be stored in paper bags or in jars. To prevent any mould forming, leave the jars open and give them an occasional shake.

Recommended varieties

Climbing French : Earliest of All. The white seeds can be used as haricots
Dwarf French : Masterpiece, The Prince
Haricot : Comtesse de Chambord, white seeds ; Rembrandt

Runner Beans

The runner bean, like the French bean, is not hardy and cannot be sown outdoors until about the middle of May, or be planted out until early June. It likes a good soil with a moisture-holding root-run, and a sunny position. If you have manure or compost to spare for this crop, it should be dug in during the autumn and winter digging.

There are several ways of growing the runner bean and each has its advantages. The traditional way is to grow the plants up poles or canes

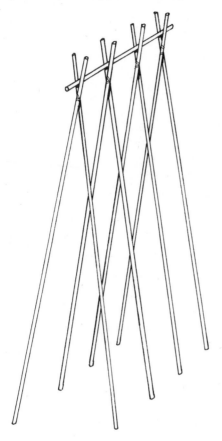

about 2.5m (8ft) long, set out in two rows 60cm (24in) apart, with 30cm (12in) between the poles. The butts should be let into the soil. The poles should be opposite each other and drawn together to cross at the top leaving a V about 20cm (8in) deep. More poles are laid in this V and the whole structure is then securely tied where the poles meet. It is worth making a good job of this as a rickety palisade may blow down in summer gales, and, if this happens, it is difficult to set it up again.

A moist root-run can be assured if a trench about 75cm (30in) wide and a spade's depth is opened out in the autumn or winter. Shovel out the loose soil and then break up the subsoil with a fork. At the bottom of the trench put a layer of newspapers and saturate them with water, then add a layer of manure or compost before filling in the trench.

Another method is to stand poles in a circle about 1–2m (3–6ft) in diameter. Sink the poles into the soil around the perimeter of the circle and then fasten them all together at the top. The advantages of this method are that the wigwams take up less room and, by not presenting an unbroken surface to the wind, are less likely to blow down.

If plants have been raised in boxes in a cold frame or greenhouse, put out one plant against each pole. Otherwise, sow one seed each side of the pole, about 5cm (2in) deep and pull one out if both grow. When the plants have climbed to the top of the poles, pinch out the growing points.

Yet another method is to grow the plants up a trellis or wire boundary fence. It does not matter if the fence is only about 1m (3ft) high. Choose a

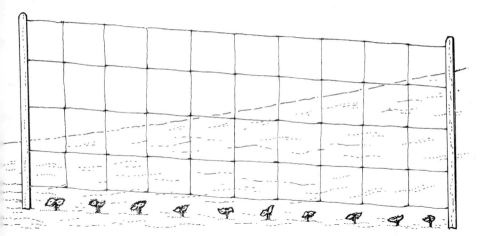

variety of medium height and let it climb the fence (as suggested for French beans). When the plants have reached the top of the fence, they will fall over on the other side and pods will form on both sides of the fence.

Runner beans may also be grown 'on the flat'. In this method the seeds are sown 5cm (2in) deep in drills 90cm (36in) apart, with the seeds 20cm (8in) apart. The plants will then grow together to form a continuous row. If the runners threaten to become entangled in the next row, pinch them back.

A development in recent years has been the introduction of the non-climbing runner bean which makes bushy plants about 45cm (18in) high. The original varieties in this field have been withdrawn because the stock has deteriorated, but other varieties are coming forward and it does seem that this type is here to stay. It is of particular value for getting an early crop under cloches.

The main pests to look out for are slugs and blackfly. Put down slug pellets when the plants are at the seedling stage, and spray with derris or malathion to control the blackfly. Never allow this pest to build up before taking counter measures—attack at the first sign of trouble.

Pick the beans regularly and strip off any older ones which may have been missed at an earlier picking. If seeds are allowed to form, the production of young beans will fall off considerably. If it is intended to save seeds for the next season, set aside a few plants for this purpose.

In hot, dry periods the flowers will sometimes fall off without setting. The cause of this is dryness at the roots, and the remedy is a thorough soaking of the root-run.

Recommended varieties

Achievement, Enorma, Prizewinner, these are all good varieties of long beans

Fry, a new white-seeded variety which has done well in dry summers

Kelvedon Marvel, of medium height, the best variety for growing on fences or along the ground

Beetroot

This is not a difficult root to grow and it will flourish in any good garden soil. Fresh manure is not advisable ; a site that was well manured for the previous crop is a good choice. The roots may be long, globe-shaped, or cylindrical. The globe beetroot is by far the most popular.

Long beetroot should be sown in April in drills 2cm (1in) deep and 38cm (15in) apart. To grow long beetroot a good depth of fertile soil is needed— not one freshly manured or the roots may fork. Thin the plants to stand 15cm (6in) apart. Care should be taken when lifting long beet as, if the roots are damaged, they will bleed. Ease them with a fork before pulling them out.

Globe beetroot can be sown from

Globe

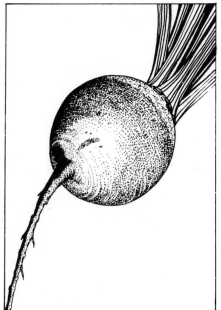

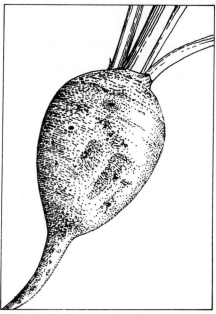

Intermediate

March to July. A March sowing will give tasty young roots for summer salads ; a July sowing, provided that the summer is not too hot and dry, will give tender roots in late autumn. There is a tendency with early sowings for some of the roots to 'bolt', ie run up to seed. These roots are hard and woody in the centre and are no use for eating. This tendency is increased if there is any check to growth. Some of the newer varieties do show some resistance to this fault.

Sow globe beetroot in drills 2cm (1in) deep and 30cm (12in) apart, and sow thinly as each seed capsule can give several seedlings. Better and earlier roots can be pulled if some thinning is done. Thin to about 5cm (2in) when they start to show, then take out every other root as soon as it is big enough to use. For good results from July sowings, it is essential to thin

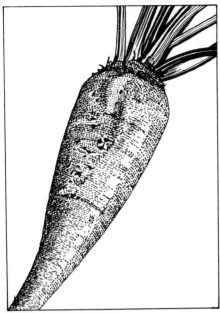
Long

attack the plants in the seedling stage and slugs can be a nuisance, especially in heavy soils. Black cotton, stretched over the seedlings as soon as they are through the soil, will keep the birds away.

Should the roots go brown and rotten inside it will indicate a deficiency of the trace element boron. The disease, which is not a common one, is known as heart-rot, and can be corrected by applying borax at 35g to 17sq m (1oz to 20sq yd).

Recommended varieties

Long beetroot : Cheltenham Green-top
Intermediate : Cylindra
Globe : Detroit, the standard globe ;
    Bolthardy, good for early sowings as
    it has some resistance to bolting

the plants to about 7cm (3in) as soon as they can be handled, as these sowings have less time in which to make good.

For use as a maincrop, globe beetroot should not be sown before the beginning of May. The intermediate or cylindrical varieties are often used as a maincrop because they give a bigger yield.

If at any time the plants do not seem to be making good progress, hoe in a dressing of agricultural salt at about 35g per metre (1oz per yard) run.

The roots can be stored during the winter months in boxes of sand or soil —a layer of beetroot, followed by a layer of soil, and so on until the box is full. For larger quantities make a little clamp in the garden, as described for potatoes (see p 45).

This vegetable is not troubled by many pests but sparrows will often

Brassicas—General

The brassica family is a very important one. In addition to the vegetables we describe loosely as 'greens'—cauliflowers, cabbages, etc—it includes radishes, turnips, kohl rabi and swedes.

The usual method of growing greens is to sow the seeds in a little nursery bed and then transplant them later. This saves valuable space as an early crop can be taken from the site reserved for greens. If, for example, early peas, lettuces or spinach are sown in rows 60cm (24in) apart, rows of Brussels sprouts can be planted between them.

Greens like a firm, fertile soil and the easiest way of achieving this is to dig in manure or compost during autumn or early winter. Leave the ground rough and then break it down in the spring.

The site for the nursery bed should be an open, sunny one, with some shelter from cold winds if possible. Rake the soil down finely, then take out shallow drills and sow the seeds thinly. Label each variety as it is sown. When the seedlings are large enough to handle, thin them to stand about 2cm (1in) apart. This thinning is often neglected but it does pay as it gives straighter and stronger plants.

When the plants are about 15cm (6in) high they can be moved to their final positions. Dull, showery weather

Transplanting

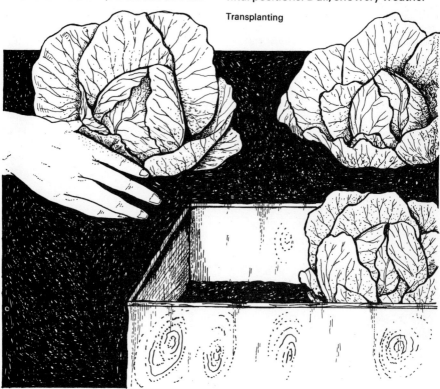

is the best time for transplanting, but unfortunately this cannot be arranged to order ! If the weather is dry, water the seed-bed well a few hours before the plants are moved so that some soil goes with them. Dig the holes to receive the plants, then fill them with water and let it drain away before the plants are put in. Plant them firmly with a trowel or dibber, then water them again.

The pests most likely to prove troublesome are the caterpillars of the cabbage-white butterfly, and the cabbage root-fly. Spraying or dusting with derris will account for the caterpillars ; for the cabbage root-fly it is vital to dust the seed drills with calomel dust and sprinkle a little of it into each planting hole. This should always be done to deter the fly from laying her eggs against the plant stem. The grubs, which hatch out from the eggs, attack the stem below ground and also the roots. The first sign of trouble is plants which wilt badly in bright sunlight. In a bad attack the plants collapse and die. Nothing can be done at the maggot stage except to pull up and burn the affected plants.

The most serious disease of the brassicas is club root, or 'finger and toe' as it is called in some districts. This causes swollen and twisted roots and inhibits growth. There is no cure but it can be controlled by using lime and calomel dust. The lime should be spread on the soil surface in January or February at 70g per sq m (2oz per sq yd). Where the soil has not been limed for some years this amount can be doubled. It helps to prevent a build-up of the fungus if a good system of crop rotation is practised, and greens are not grown on the same site too often.

Club root

Root-fly

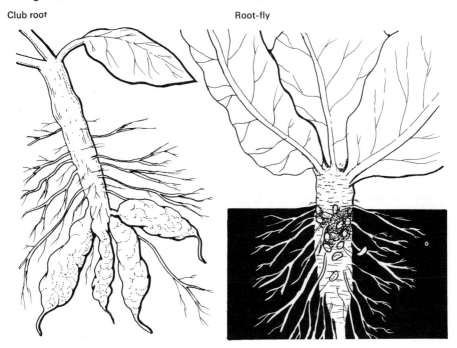

Brassicas—
Brussels Sprouts

Because of its long period of cropping, the Brussels sprout ranks high among the brassicas. By using an early and late variety, sprouts may be picked throughout the autumn and winter. Moreover, as they freeze so well you need never be caught out by a glut and you may be able to freeze some for year-round use.

The seeds should be sown in the nursery bed in the second half of March, or early in April. An earlier start can be made if a cold frame or cloches are available. Sow the seeds directly into the frame bed or in boxes 10–15cm (4–6in) deep. An ordinary seed tray is not deep enough to give good root development.

The advice given in the section on Brassicas—General regarding the plants' need for a firm, fertile soil applies particularly to Brussels sprouts. Loose soil is one of the reasons why

Blown sprouts

sprouts 'blow'—ie develop loose rosettes of leaves instead of tight buttons. The advice about pests given in Brassicas—General also holds good.

When planting out, a minimum distance of 60cm (24in) should be allowed between plants and rows, but if space is at a premium, the dwarf or half-tall varieties may be restricted to 53cm (21in) between plants. The tall varieties cannot be expected to give good results under 60cm (24in) and will get more light and air if the distance between the rows can be increased to 75cm (30in).

Some form of staking may be necessary for the tall varieties, particularly those planted in exposed positions. The plants facing the prevailing wind are vulnerable, as are those growing at the corners of the plot. One way of giving them better anchorage is to draw up a little soil around the base of the stems.

When the plants are established, a dressing of a good general fertilizer can be given at 70g per sq m (2oz per sq yd). In the autumn take off any of the lower leaves which have turned yellow and put them on the compost heap.

The cabbage-like head of the plant is also edible and is preferred by some people to the sprouts, but do not take it too early as its real purpose is to protect the developing sprouts. In bad weather, without the protection of the leafy head, the buttons may rot. Late February or early March is a good time to cut out the top ; its removal then will help the topmost sprouts to develop.

Always pick sprouts from the bottom upwards and either cut or snap them off cleanly, close to the stem. In April

any remaining buttons will burst open and send up leafy shoots. These, if left alone will grow on to form flowers and seeds. Cut them and use them when they are a few inches in length. Do not allow the shoots to flower for it is at this stage that the plants are taking most nourishment from the soil.

When the last sprouts have been gathered, chop the plants up with a spade and dig in all the green stuff. The roots take a long time to rot and are better burnt.

Recommended varieties

Early : Early Half-tall, September to Christmas ; Peer Gynt (F1 hybrid), medium height

Late : Citadel (F1 hybrid), medium height ; Cambridge No5, tall

Brassicas—Cabbages

Cabbages are easy to grow and are in season all the year round. This makes them one of the most valuable members of the brassica family. Although they appreciate a good, fertile medium they are less demanding in their soil requirements than Brussels sprouts or cauliflowers.

Spring Cabbages

These are sown in July and August for maturing from April to June. It is a good plan to make two sowings—one about mid-July and another three weeks later. If the first sowing fails, there is always the other one to fall back on. The July sowing will form plants to put out in September; from an August sowing plants will be ready for transplanting early in October. Spring cabbages make a good follow-on crop to potatoes.

The smaller varieties should be given 30cm (12in) between plants and 45cm (18in) between the rows; the larger varieties should be 45cm (18in) between plants and 60cm (24in) between the rows. If these distances between the plants are halved, every other plant can be taken out in March for use as 'spring greens'.

Spring cabbages have a distinctive, nutty flavour of their own and come in at a time when other greens are scarce. They do not suffer from club root (which is not active during the winter months) but may need protection from birds, especially wood pigeons (a net is ideal), and from cabbage root-fly. Fresh manure should not be used and fertilizers should not be given until the spring when a little nitro-chalk —about 70g per sq m (2oz per sq yd)— will give them a boost.

Summer and Autumn Cabbages

These are sown with the other brassicas in the nursery bed in March or April and are planted out in May and June, their season being July to September. They include both round (R) and pointed (P) types. A later sowing about mid-May will prolong the season until October.

The smaller cabbages in this group will need 38–45cm (15–18in) between plants and 53cm (21in) between the

Planting out red cabbage

rows. The larger cabbages should be given 53cm (21in) between plants and 60cm (24in) between the rows.

Round cabbage

Winter Cabbages

The winter cabbages are hardier and slower to mature than the summer ones. They crop from October to February. They should be sown in the nursery bed during April, and be planted out in June or July, 60cm (24in) apart, in all directions. The winter cabbages will stand for some time without splitting. If they are dug up with the roots intact and hung head downwards in a cool, airy shed or cellar, they will remain in good condition for weeks. The variety January King, available from December to February, is worth a special mention as it is in a class of its own. A cross between a cabbage and a savoy it is very hardy and has a good flavour. Some seedsmen list it with the savoys.

Savoy Cabbages

The savoys are the hardiest of all cabbages and can be used from November to April, according to variety. Their leaves are darker than those of ordinary cabbages and are more crimped and curled. They stand well without splitting.

Sow the seeds in the nursery seed-bed in April for the early kinds and in May for the later ones.

Red Cabbages

Although red cabbages are used mainly for pickling they can also be prepared as a vegetable. They need a long season of growth and should be sown in the nursery seed-bed in March. Alternatively, for a better start, sow a few seeds under a cloche in February. The best red cabbages of all come from a sowing made with the spring cabbages in July or August. Planted out in late September or early October, 60cm (24in) apart, in all directions, they will stand through the winter. Their leaves are tough and birds do not usually attack them.

Recommended varieties

Spring Cabbages : April or Wheeler's Imperial are a good, small variety ; Flower of Spring, a late, large cabbage

Summer Cabbages : Greyhound (P) and Primo (R) are two early, small varieties ; Winnigstadt (P) and Emerald Cross (R) are later and larger

Winter Cabbages : Christmas Drumhead, dwarf and compact ; Holland Winter White and Winter Monarch, two of the best white cabbages for winter use

Savoy Cabbages : Best of All, early and good ; Ormskirk Late, one of the best late varieties

Red Cabbages : Niggerhead, medium size ; Large Blood Red

Brassicas—
Cauliflowers and
Cauliflower Broccoli

A good, white cauliflower is always a welcome addition to the vegetable supply. Unfortunately, it is not one of the easiest vegetables to grow well. A good, fertile soil is needed, well supplied with humus. A medium loam is ideal, but cauliflowers will do well on heavier soils provided that the drainage is good. They can be divided naturally into two groups : the true cauliflowers which mature during summer and autumn, and the cauliflower broccoli which is in season from February to May, according to the area. These are now usually listed in seed catalogues as 'winter' cauliflowers.

To obtain cauliflowers in June and July it is necessary to raise the plants under glass in a cold greenhouse or frame by sowing in boxes in January or February. An alternative, where cloches are available, is to sow under cloches in September and keep the plants covered throughout the winter. Whichever method is employed, the plants must be well hardened off before they are planted out in the open.

For heading in late summer and autumn, the seeds should be sown in the nursery seed-bed along with the other brassicas. Varieties maturing in August and September can be sown in April, but those for October and November heading should not be sown until about the middle of May. The early varieties should have 45cm (18in) between the plants and 53cm (21in) between the rows ; later varieties 53cm (21in) between the plants and 60cm (24in) between the rows.

In transplanting cauliflowers be careful to minimize the check to growth. If the soil is dry, water the seed-bed well a few hours before the plants are lifted so that some soil can be taken with the roots. Cauliflowers which suffer a bad check are liable to retaliate by producing their curds prematurely when they are no bigger than egg-cups. This practice is known as 'buttoning'.

A check to growth may also occur if the plants dry out. Keep them well supplied with water in dry weather. Feeding with liquid manure is always a good thing.

Cauliflower broccoli are hardier and generally easier to manage than the true cauliflower, but the curds can be damaged by frost. For this reason, except in frost-free areas, there is not much point in going for the earliest varieties which head in January and

Buttoned cauliflower

Protecting curds from frost

February. For most parts the season is from March to June.

These cauliflowers need a long period of growth and the seeds should be sown in April or May, for transplanting in June or July. They can often be used as a follow-on crop to potatoes or early peas. If this is done, simply prick the soil over, a few inches deep, with a fork and then rake it down again. A sprinkling of a general fertilizer can be given—not exceeding 70g per sq m (2oz per sq yd)—but no other feeding, as the object is to grow a plant hardy enough to stand the winter. Give the plants 60cm (24in), all ways.

The curds of cauliflowers can be yellowed by bright sunlight or blackened by frost. Snap a few leaves over the developing curd of summer cauliflowers when it becomes visible in order to protect it. The inner leaves of cauliflower broccoli fold over to protect the curd, but if there is a likelihood of frost before the curds are ready for cutting, it is always a good plan to snap one or two of the outer leaves over as well.

Recommended varieties

June and July heading :
    Early Snowball, Dominant
August and September : All the Year
    Round, South Pacific
October and November : Autumn
    Giant, Canberra
March and April : Leamington, St
    George
May and June : Royal Oak, Late Queen

Brassicas—Sprouting Broccoli, Calabrese and Kales

Sprouting Broccoli

This brassica does not form a central head but a number of sideshoots, each of which carries a small flower like a tiny cauliflower. It is available in two forms, purple and white, and crops during March and April. The white form is believed by many gardeners to have better flavour than the purple, but it is not quite so hardy.

Seeds of sprouting broccoli should be sown in the nursery seed-bed in late March or April, for transplanting to stand 60cm (24in) apart in all directions. A soil in good heart in an open, sunny position should be chosen, but not one freshly manured as the plants need to be grown hard to stand through the winter. There is no need to wait until the flower head shows; the shoots can be taken as soon as they are long enough to pick.

Sprouting broccoli

Calabrese

Another form of sprouting broccoli is known as calabrese. This is an all-green type which matures from October to December. Some varieties have a large, central head, rather like a cauliflower, which is followed by sideshoots. In others the head is smaller, with more sideshoots. Calabrese freezes well, and large quantities of it are now being grown for the frozen-food trade.

To grow calabrese sow the seeds in April and then move the young plants into their final quarters in June or July. Give them 45cm (18in) between plants and 60cm (24in) between the rows. They can often be used as a follow-on crop to earlier vegetables. Where this is done put down a general fertilizer at about 70g per sq m (2oz per sq yd) and prick it into the top few inches of soil with a fork.

Kales

Last but not least among the brassicas are the kales, the hardiest members of the family. Although they will naturally do best in a good, fertile soil, they are not as demanding in their soil requirements as Brussels sprouts or cauliflowers. They, too, can be used as a follow-on crop to earlier vegetables.

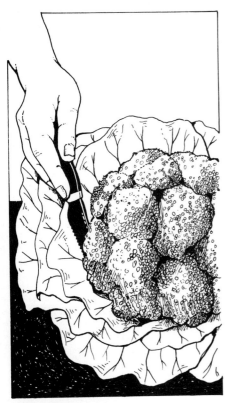

Cutting calabrese heads

Scotch kale

Sow the seeds in the nursery seed-bed during April or early May and plant out in late June or July. There are several types of this vegetable, some with densely-curled, dark-green leaves, and others with plain leaves. The dwarf Scotch kales should be given 45cm (18in) between plants and 60cm (24in) between the rows; the others should be 60cm (24in) apart in all directions. An exception to this is Hungry Gap kale which needs rather different treatment as the seeds should be sown in June or July in the bed where the plants are to mature. Sow in shallow drills 60cm (24in) apart, and then thin the seedlings to stand 30cm (12in) apart. This is the hardiest of all the kales and the latest to mature.

Recommended varieties

Sprouting Broccoli : Early White, Late White ; Early Purple, Late Purple

Calabrese : Green Comet (F1 hybrid), large central head, followed by sideshoots ; Autumn Spear, an abundance of green shoots

Kales : Scotch (tall and dwarf), densely curled ; Thousand-headed, plain leaves ; Pentland Brig (F1 hybrid), a cross between the curly and plain-leaved types

Carrots

Most vegetable gardeners want to grow carrots, but it must be admitted that this is not one of the easiest vegetables to grow successfully. Few gardeners have ideal carrot soil, which is a light to medium loam, well worked to a good depth and moisture retentive. However, much can be done by taking a little extra trouble and using the right varieties. Light soils can be enriched by digging in manure or compost during the winter months, and heavy soils can be lightened with the addition of coarse sand or weathered ashes forked into the top 15cm (6in) of soil. On soils which do not have a good depth of fertile soil, grow only the stump-rooted varieties.

Carrots can be sown at any time from March to July, or earlier than March if there is a cold frame or cloches to give protection. For the earliest sowings, use the shorthorn or early stump-rooted varieties, and come back to them for the July sowing which is designed to give young carrots for pulling in autumn.

Maincrop carrots for storing should not be sown earlier than the middle of

Thinning seedling carrots

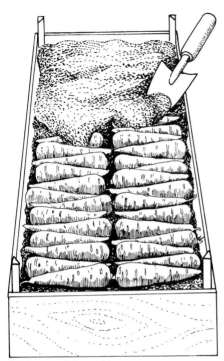
Storing carrots in sand box

carrots. This little creature lays her eggs along the carrot rows. From the eggs hatch little maggots which burrow into the soil and then tunnel into the developing roots. In a severe attack the roots can be ruined. The presence of the grubs can be detected by changes in the foliage which loses its green lustre and turns a dull, reddish brown. Unfortunately, by that time not much can be done. Control lies in keeping the fly away. One method of control is to dust the seed-drills with a good seed dressing or Gamma/BHC dust, and to repeat this when the seedlings are a few inches high. Bromophos is another preparation recommended as a control.

In an open autumn carrots will continue to grow until November. While they can be left in the ground all winter, it is better to lift and store them. Heavy rains may cause the roots to split and they will be a prey to slugs, millipedes or wireworms. They store well in layers, head to tail, in boxes of sand or soil, or in a little clamp in the garden.

May, up until early June, as these later sowings have more chance of missing the destructive carrot-fly. Where there is sufficient depth of soil to grow long carrots, these give the heaviest crops of all.

Sowing of all varieties should be done in drills not more than 13mm ($\frac{1}{2}$in) deep and 25–30cm (10–12in) apart. Sow *thinly*. Some thinning may still have to be done, for if the seedlings are crowded in the row, many of them will never make usable roots, and it is better to remove them in the early stages. Thin the early varieties to about 2cm (1in) and the maincrops to 5–8cm (2–3in), and put the thinnings on the compost heap. Never leave them lying about on the soil as the carrot smell may attract the fly.

The carrot-fly is the scourge of

Recommended varieties

Early carrots : Early Horn, Early Nantes
Maincrop carrots : James Scarlet Intermediate, Chantenay Red Cored
Long carrots : St Valery, Autumn King

Celery and Celeriac

Trench celery needs a rich soil, well supplied with humus, and plenty of water. Unless these conditions can be given, it is better to stick to the self-blanching celery, which is easier to grow but not such good quality.

Celery and celeriac need a long period of growth and the seeds should be sown in a seed-pan during February. A gently-heated greenhouse is ideal for raising celery plants, but if this is not available put the seed-pan in the sunny window of a warm room, and turn the pan daily when the seedlings have appeared. When they have formed their first true leaves, prick them off into boxes and put them in a cold frame or under a cloche. By June or early July they will be ready for transplanting.

For trench celery, take out a trench 45cm (18in) wide and a spade's depth. Shovel out the loose soil and then break up the subsoil with a fork. Put in a good layer of manure or compost, then return most of the soil, leaving the trench a few inches deep. As the soil is returned, mix in some bonemeal or weathered soot (ie soot which has been stored for several months).

When the plants are ready for moving, put them out in the trench in two rows 23cm (9in) apart in all directions. The plants should be opposite each other in the rows, not staggered. From then on, until earthing-up begins, see that they never lack water. It is difficult to overwater celery.

Trench celery needs blanching before it can be eaten, and this work is done in several stages by drawing soil up round the stems. When the plants have made good growth (usually about mid-August) cut off any suckers, yellow leaves and small leaves that would be buried by the soil, then draw the stems together and make a loose tie with soft string. Holding the plant with one hand, take the soil from the sides of the trench and sweep it up round the stems. Take care that the soil does not fall into the hearts of the plants, or they may rot. Repeat this

Celery plants in trench

process every two or three weeks until about the end of September when most of the growth will have been made.

After the final earthing, only the tips of the plants should be visible above the bank of soil. Pat the sides of the bank smooth with the back of the spade. In three or four weeks blanching will be completed. To dig the sticks, start at one end of the double row and remove the bank until the whole of the stick is visible, then thrust the spade well down under the root.

An alternative method which can be recommended is to wait until most of the growth has been made and then tie cardboard collars round the plants before earthing them up. This keeps the sticks cleaner and makes it more difficult for slugs to get at them. It is best to use corrugated cardboard.

There are white, pink, and red varieties of trench celery. The white is not quite so hardy as the other two and should be eaten first.

Self-blanching celery, as the name implies, does its own blanching. To do this successfully it should be planted in blocks and not in long rows. Put the plants out 20cm (8in) apart, in all directions. The plants on the edges of the block will need some help and this can be given, either by earthing them up, or by packing boards, straw, or short litter against them. This type of celery is less hardy than trench celery and generally needs to be used up by Christmas.

Celeriac, or turnip-rooted celery, forms a swollen root which has the true celery flavour. It may be used grated in salads or as a vegetable. It does not need blanching. The plants go out in rows 45cm (18in) apart, with 30cm (12in) between the plants. The only attention necessary is to cut off any suckers or lateral shoots from the roots as they swell. The roots are hardy and can be left outside.

The two pests of the celery family are slugs and the celery-fly. To combat the slugs sprinkle slug pellets around the plants, and include some in the soil when earthing-up. Grubs from the eggs of the celery-fly burrow into the leaves, leaving shiny, blistery trails. This saps the strength of the plants. Spray with Lindex or malathion to control them.

Recommended varieties

Trench celery : Giant Red, Giant White, Clayworth Pink
Self-blanching: Lathom Self-blanching
Celeriac : Globus

Trench celery with cardboard collar

Leeks

The leek is a useful vegetable as it comes in during winter and early spring. It is easy to grow and not prone to pests or diseases. It likes a soil enriched with humus, and given this will do well in heavy or light conditions.

Leeks can be bought at planting time from nurserymen or garden centres, but they are quite easy to raise from seeds. These should be sown in a seed-bed in late March or early April. Sow the seeds thinly in shallow drills 25cm (10in) apart.

Planting out can be done from June to August, and this means that leeks are often used as a follow-on crop to earlier vegetables. If the ground was manured for a previous crop, it will be enough to fork it over and add a general fertilizer at 70g per sq m (2oz per sq yd). If it was not manured, then dig it over and put in some well rotted manure or compost, burying this in the bottom of each trench as leeks are deep rooting.

The plants can be moved when they are about 15cm (6in) high. Ease them first with a fork, then pull them up and sort them. Reject any plants which are not straight, and any which have a short stem. Trim the leaves of the chosen plants by about half, and the roots likewise. This makes for easier planting.

To plant leeks, make a hole deep enough to take the plant up to its lowest leaves, drop it in, trickle a little soil over the roots, then fill the hole with water. The remainder of the hole will fill in when hoeing takes place. Allow 20cm (8in) between the plants. The distance between the rows will depend on whether the plants are to be earthed-up or not. They can be planted as close as 30cm (12in), but if soil is to be drawn up to them to give a greater length of blanched stem, a minimum of 45cm (18in) will be required. Choose a dry day in October to do the earthing and draw the soil up under the lowest leaves.

The two main periods of growth are in autumn and early spring, but unless the weather is severe, leeks will make some growth all through the winter. By May any remaining plants should be dug as they will then begin to produce their seed heads.

Leeks are perfectly hardy and can remain in the ground all winter. The only problem may be that during severe frost it will be difficult to dig them. This can be avoided if one or two rows are mulched with peat or straw which will absorb most of the frost.

Although leeks *may* be attacked by the onion-fly or onion white rot (see Onions), they rarely are. If they are not grown on the same site too often they are generally free from pests or diseases, which is another point in their favour.

Recommended varieties
The Lyon, Musselburgh, Marble Pillar

(*From the top*) planting; watering; earthing up to blanch stems

Lettuces, Outdoor Cucumbers and Gherkins

Lettuces

There are three types of lettuces in general cultivation : cabbage, cos, and non-hearting. Lettuces with a cabbage-like head may be either smooth, or crisp and curled. Cos lettuce has oval leaves which fold over to make a pointed heart. The non-hearting lettuce forms a loose head of curly leaves which can be picked as required.

Apart from the winter months, when a heated greenhouse is needed, it is not difficult to grow lettuce. The introduction of improved varieties and the use of cloches, which are excellent for lettuce, has extended the season at both ends. And the lettuce is not particularly fussy in its soil requirements. It does not mind a heavy soil provided that the drainage is good. On light, hungry soils it may bolt in dry weather (go to seed prematurely), but this tendency can be overcome by forking good compost or peat into the top few inches of soil.

Early lettuces can be obtained by raising the plants in boxes in a cold frame or under cloches. If cloches are placed in position some weeks beforehand to warm the soil, a sowing can be made outdoors in January or February. Lettuces are hardier than is often supposed. The seeds should be sown in shallow drills 25–30cm (10–12in) apart. Outdoor sowings without protection can be made from March to July.

Lettuces for maturing during the summer months should be sown in April and May. This is also the main season for sowing cos lettuce.

In July, sowings can be made for autumn use, and for these we turn back to the early varieties. Tom Thumb, a small cabbage lettuce, can be sown well into August and will still mature before winter, especially if it is cloched in September.

Certain varieties can be sown in August for overwintering which will mature in early spring. Their success will depend to a large extent on the severity of the winter. A sunny position, sheltered from cold winds, should be chosen for them.

A better and more certain way of obtaining lettuces in spring is to sow them in September and cover them with cloches a month later. Make a preliminary thinning to 5–8cm (2–3in) when the plants are big enough to handle, then thin them again in February, this time to 12–15cm (5–6in). The February thinnings can be transplanted to give a later row. In April, take out every other plant for early use.

Most lettuces should be thinned out to stand 25–30cm (10–12in) apart, but Tom Thumb and Little Gem do not need more than 15cm (6in). Lettuces maturing during July and August will do better if sown in the lee of taller crops which will give them some shade for part of the day.

Birds and slugs are the worst enemies of lettuce, but bird damage can be prevented by stringing black cotton over the plants. Botrytis may cause a problem in frames or under cloches. This disease, known also as 'brown rot', causes the plants to rot off at soil level. The best safeguard against it is to give plenty of ventilation so that a good circulation of air is maintained.

Ridge Cucumbers and Gherkins

The outdoor or ridge cucumber can be raised in pots in a cool greenhouse by sowing two seeds, 13mm ($\frac{1}{2}$in) deep in a pot about the middle of April. If both seeds grow, pull one out. The plants may also be raised in a similar way in a sunny window. By early June, when the risk of frost has passed, they will be ready for planting out.

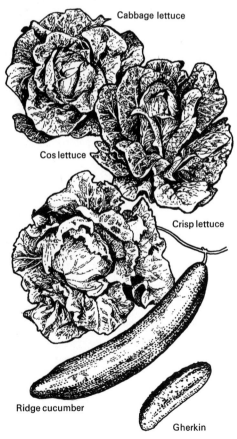

Cabbage lettuce

Cos lettuce

Crisp lettuce

Ridge cucumber

Gherkin

An alternative method is to sow the seeds directly into the soil during the middle of May. Sow three seeds in a triangle and thin them to the strongest plant. The planting sites should be prepared by digging holes 45cm (18in) square and 30cm (12in) deep. Half-fill these with manure or good compost, then return the soil. This will leave the plants on a slight mound. The prepared sites should be 75cm (30in) apart.

When the plants have made three pairs of leaves pinch out the growing points. This will make them produce lateral shoots on which the fruits form. It is not necessary to remove the male flowers. The crop will be largely at the mercy of the weather, but, if barn cloches can be used to cover the plants for at least part of their growth, the chance of success will be much greater.

The cultivation of the gherkin is the same as that of the ridge cucumber. Pick the fruits when they are a few inches long and the plants will go on producing for weeks.

Recommended varieties

Lettuces : (cabbage varieties unless otherwise stated)
For use in summer and autumn : All the Year Round, Buttercrunch, Webb's Wonderful, Unrivalled, Tom Thumb, Lobjoits Green Cos, Little Gem (small cos)
For overwintering without protection : Arctic King, Valdor
For overwintering with protection : Suzan (also listed as Hilde), Premier, Winter Density (cos)
Ridge Cucumbers : Baton Vert, Burpless
Gherkins : Venlo Pickling

Onions

Onions like a rich, firm soil. A medium to heavy loam suits them best, but they will do well in lighter soils provided that there is a good reserve of humus.

There are three main ways of growing onions : growing from seed in August for overwintering ; growing from seed in early spring, and growing from onion sets.

The August sowing should be sited on a strip which was manured for the previous crop, eg early potatoes. No fertilizer should be given at this stage as sappy growth is not wanted. Simply fork the soil through, a few inches deep, then rake it down again and sow the seeds in drills about 13mm ($\frac{1}{2}$in) deep and 25–30cm (10–12in) apart. Keep the plants clean by hoeing and weeding whenever possible. In the spring thin the seedlings to 10cm (4in) apart, or 15cm (6in) if larger bulbs are needed, and use the thinnings as 'spring onions'. Liquid manure, at fortnightly intervals, is a good help when the bulbs begin to form.

Care should be taken in choosing varieties for this sowing as some varieties are quite unsuitable. The new Japanese onions are rapidly gaining favour and have so far withstood British winters successfully.

For sowing in spring the ground should be dug and manured in autumn or early winter so that it has time to settle down before sowing. In March or early April (March, if possible), rake the soil down into a fine tilth. Larger bulbs can be obtained by sowing in boxes in a lightly heated greenhouse in January, or in a cold greenhouse in

Planting sets

February. These plants can be put out in April.

Onion sets are tiny bulbs in an arrested state of development which are planted 10–15cm (4–6in) apart, in rows 25–30cm (10–12in) apart, and this is now the most popular method of growing onions. The easiest way of planting them is to draw out shallow drills and then make a little depression with the tip of the trowel. Push the soil back so that the bulbs are just covered.

Spring onions   Globe onion

This method avoids trouble from the birds, which are likely to pull the bulbs out again if any part is showing.

The popular salad onions can be sown in rows 15cm (6in) apart in August and September for spring use, or March to May for summer use. These should be pulled up in the green state. Pickling onions should be sown thickly in a broad row 15cm (6in) wide in April. Salad and pickling onions do not need a rich soil.

The worst onion pest is the onion-fly, which lays her eggs against the young plants. White maggots come from the eggs and burrow into the bulbs. Yellow, sickly-looking foliage is a sign of their presence. There is no cure at the maggot stage. Calomel dust, sprinkled up the sides of the rows at the seedling stage, helps to keep the fly away. August-sown plants and sets, although not immune to this trouble, are less likely to be attacked.

Yellow, sickly plants may also be a sign of onion white rot. In this disease a white mould attacks the base of the bulb. Affected plants should be pulled up and burnt, and onions should not be grown again on that site for several years. Fortunately, the disease is not widespread.

Onions are ready for harvesting when the tips of the leaves turn yellow and then flop over. Ease the bulbs with a fork before pulling them out, then dry them thoroughly in the sunshine. An onion rope can be made by hanging up a length of stout string and then tying the onions to it, beginning at the bottom and working up. Alternatively, store them in shallow boxes in a light, cool place.

Recommendeded varieties

August sowing : Reliance, Solidity ;
    Japanese varieties : Empress Yellow,
    Imai
Spring sowing : Ailsa Craig,
    Bedfordshire Champion
Sets : Suttgarter Giant, Sturon
Salad onions : White Lisbon
Pickling onions : Paris Silverskin

37

Parsnips

The parsnip is a good winter vegetable, hardy, and easy to grow. It also makes good wine. It will grow in most soils but, like most roots, should not be grown in freshly-manured soil.

It is sometimes recommended that parsnips should be sown in February, but the ground is often too wet for this. A March sowing is just as good and even April sowings, if made in the first half of the month, will give roots large enough for kitchen use.

Sow the seeds in shallow drills about 13mm ($\frac{1}{2}$in) deep and 38cm (15in) apart. There are two methods of sowing. One is to trickle the seeds all the way along the drill and then thin the plants to 15cm (6in) apart when they are big enough to handle. In the other method, known as 'station'

sowing, a few seeds are sown at 15cm (6in) intervals. The seedlings from these are thinned to leave the strongest plant at each station.

The advantages of the second method are that less seed is required and that there is room to sow a few radishes between the clusters of parsnip seeds. This is to mark the rows for hoeing. Parsnips are slow to germinate and take weeks to come through. The radishes come through first and, by marking the rows, enable hoeing to be done before weeds get the upper hand.

Keep the plants clean by hoeing and weeding; no special cultivation is needed. As the tops attain their full growth, light will be excluded from between the rows and no further weeding will be necessary.

The roots are ready for digging when the foliage has died down. There is no

'Trickle' sowing   'Station' sowing

point in digging them earlier than this for most gardeners agree that the roots are sweeter when they have been touched by frost. To get them out intact dig out a spadeful of soil from against each root, then put the spade into the hole and thrust it well down and under.

Parsnips are completely hardy and can be left in the ground all winter. Should severe weather threaten to make conditions impossible for digging, lift a few roots and store them in a box of sand or soil. By the end of March or early in April the plants, being biennial, will begin to make fresh growth. It is time then to dig up any roots which are left and put them, with soil mixed among them, in a shady corner until they can be used up.

The only trouble likely to be encountered with parsnips is canker. This fungus disease causes the roots to crack, usually at the shoulders, and then produce brown patches which may go rotten. There is no cure. There is some reason to believe that April sowings are less likely to be attacked. Where the disease is prevalent—but many gardeners never see it—it is worth sowing late and growing a variety that has some resistance to canker.

Recommended varieties

Avonresister, a small, conical root which has some resistance to canker
Improved Hollow Crown, long, well-shaped roots
Offenham, stump-rooted, suitable for shallow soils

Digging parsnips

Peas

Peas will grow in most soils provided that they have a good humus content. Where the ground was dug and manured during the winter, no other preparation will be necessary, except to give a dressing of lime over the digging at about 70g per sq m (2oz per sq yd). Peas like lime.

There is a wide range of varieties to choose from, dwarf, medium and tall. The dwarf varieties are the most popular, no doubt because they are the least trouble.

Sowings can take place in October or November, and from March to the end of June. In most areas the autumn sowing will need some protection. A row of cloches is ideal. Where cloches can be used, a February sowing is also possible. For these sowings it is customary to use a round-seeded variety rather than a wrinkled one. The round-seeded peas are hardier than the wrinkled ones but are not of such good flavour.

For sowings in March and April choose an early, wrinkled variety. Maincrop varieties are sown in May. For the June sowings, which have only a limited time in which to mature, return to the early varieties.

There are two methods of sowing. One is to take out a drill about 5cm (2in) deep with the corner of a draw hoe and sow the seeds thinly along the bottom of the drill. The other is to scoop out a trench about 5cm (2in) deep with the spade and sow the peas in three lines, with all the peas being about 5cm (2in) apart.

For the tall varieties it is best to take out a trench 38cm (15in) wide. Break up the subsoil and put in a layer of manure or compost before returning the soil. Do this work several months in advance of sowing. Although the tall peas are more trouble, they are worth a place as the peas are large and of superb flavour. April and May are the months for sowing.

The distance between the rows of peas should be about the same as their height, eg plants 45cm (18in) high will need that distance between the rows. However, where space is precious (as it is for most of us) some savings can be made. Varieties 75cm (30in) in height will do well enough with 60cm (24in) between the rows, and those 122–152cm (48–60in) in height can be given 107cm (42in) between the rows. Summer lettuces can be intercropped between the rows of tall peas and will benefit from the shade given by the taller plants.

Although dwarf peas are supposed not to need staking, it helps to keep them cleaner and easier to pick if twiggy sticks are pushed in on each side of the row when the plants are about 15cm (6in) high. For the tall varieties some form of support is essential. Brushwood is ideal but difficult to obtain. Large mesh netting for supporting peas and beans is a good substitute. When netting is used for peas, run it up *both* sides of the row so that the peas climb up inside the netting and grow through it. This makes it impossible for summer winds to blow the plants off the netting. Make sure it is firmly fixed.

Birds love the tender green shoots of peas and can soon play havoc with a crop. Strands of black cotton,

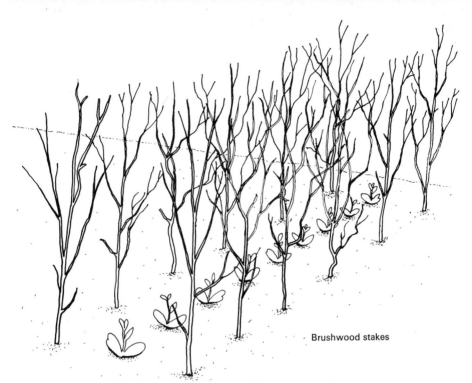

Brushwood stakes

suspended just above the seedlings when they come through, will prevent this damage. Run further strands across as the peas grow. The other menace at the seedling stage is the pea weevil, which bites holes in the young leaves. This can be controlled by spraying or dusting with derris.

Grubby peas are the work of the pea moth. They can be prevented by spraying or dusting with derris when the flowers appear, and again about ten days later. Do this in the late evening so that the bees are not harmed.

When picking peas take care that the bines are not twisted or broken. If this happens the upper pods will not fill. The bine should be held in one hand while the pods are picked off with the other.

When the crop has been gathered, run the hoe along the row to cut off the haulms, which can then be put on the compost heap. The roots of peas are rich in nitrogen and should be left in the soil.

Recommended varieties

(The height of the variety is given in brackets. All have wrinkled seeds unless otherwise stated.)
October/November sowings : Feltham First (round seeded), 45cm (18in)
March/April sowings : Kelvedon Wonder, 45cm (18in) ; Early Onward, 60cm (24in)
April/May sowings : Onward, 60cm (24in) ; The Lincoln, 60cm (24in) ; Miracle, 137cm (54in) ; Lord Chancellor, 122cm (48in)
June sowings : Little Marvel, 45cm (18in)

Potatoes

Cultivation

Potatoes can be grown in most soils. Light soils need the addition of plenty of humus, or the plants may die during a dry period. Heavy soils can be made more open by the addition of strawy manure or rough compost. Potatoes like a loose medium into which they can thrust their stolons (underground shoots on which the tubers form).

Early potatoes are planted in March and April and crop from June to August. Late varieties are planted in April and May and mature from September to October. If the vegetable plot is a small one it is wise to concentrate on the earlies.

Potatoes are propagated by planting a tuber of the previous year's growth. These are referred to as 'seed' potatoes. They may be either 'once grown', ie tubers saved from your own crop, or 'new' seed, ie new Scotch or Irish stock bought through a seedsman.

Unfortunately, the potato is subject to a number of virus diseases which are spread largely by greenfly. The professional seed-growing areas are at a high altitude where greenfly cannot work, and these stocks are certified 'virus free'. It is reasonably safe to save some tubers from the new seed of the earlies, which have a shorter growing period, but risky to save them from the later varieties.

Whether the seed tubers are new or once grown they should be 'chitted' before being planted. This is done by taking a shallow box and tilting it at one end. The tubers are then stood on end in the box with the 'eye' end uppermost.

When filled, the boxes should be stored in a light, cool and frost-proof place. Strong, young shoots will grow from the eyes. Chitting gives the tubers an early start and enables any dud tubers to be picked out before planting. Once-grown tubers can be set up as early as January or February (these give the earliest crops) ; new seed as soon as you have bought it.

There are several methods of planting. One of the most popular is to put your garden-line down across the plot and, with the back of the spade close up to the line, chip out a trench 10–15cm (4–6in) deep. Plant the tubers upright in the bottom of the trench, and fill it in with the soil thrown forward from the next trench.

Another method is to plant with the trowel. Draw out shallow drills where the rows are to be, make holes with a trowel and drop the tuber in. The advantages of this method are that any manure or greenstuff which has been dug in is not disturbed, and that

Planting in trenches

uniform planting is assured because the holes can be adjusted to the size of the tubers.

A more modern method is to use strips of black polythene 60cm (24in) wide. The tubers are planted just beneath the soil surface and the polythene is laid out above them. Soil on the edges of the polythene keeps it in place. When the shoots can be seen pushing at the polythene, slits are made with a knife and the shoots are drawn through. Using this method there is no need for hoeing or earthing-up as the polythene acts as a mulch. The tubers form beneath the sheet or just inside the soil.

Early varieties should be planted with 30cm (12in) between the tubers and 60cm (24in) between the rows. Late varieties need 38cm (15in) between the tubers and 60–68cm (24–27in) between the rows.

Potatoes are not frost hardy and, if frost threatens any shoots which have come through, they should be covered

Planting in holes

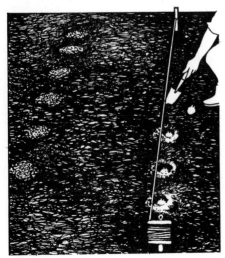

with newspapers, plant-pots or cloches. If the worst happens and the growth is blackened by frost, the tubers will send out fresh shoots, but the crop will be later and possibly smaller.

When hoeing the young plants, do not hoe too deeply or some of the underground stolons may be cut off. When the plants are about 15cm (6in) high, they should be earthed-up. This is done by standing between two rows, facing the row to be earthed. Reach out over the row with the hoe and, with a steady chopping movement, draw the soil up under the leaves of the plants. Turn at the end of the row and do the other side. This leaves the tubers in a ridge. The object of earthing-up is to prevent the tubers from pushing up into the sunlight. Tubers greened by the sun are unfit for human consumption.

No further cultivation is necessary with the possible exception of spraying the late varieties against blight. This fungus disease produces browny-black patches on the leaves, and these spread quickly, destroying the haulms. The spores, if washed into the soil, spread disease to the tubers. Blight is at its worst in damp, humid weather in July and August. If its presence is known or suspected in the area, spray the plants thoroughly with a copper-based solution such as Bordeaux mixture.

Recommended varieties

Earlies : Arran Pilot, white kidney ; Home Guard, white oval ; Pentland Javelin, white oval

Lates : Majestic, white kidney ; Pentland Crown, white oval ; Desiree, red kidney

Potatoes and Jerusalem Artichokes

Harvesting and Storing Potatoes

Early potatoes are dug as required while the haulms are still green. If any part of the crop is not dug at this stage it can still be used after the haulms have died off, the only difference being that the tubers will no longer scrape.

Late varieties are not harvested until the haulms have died. This process begins with a yellowing of the lower leaves, followed by the gradual browning of the leaves and stems.

To lift the tubers, put the fork in at the side of the ridge—not across the ridge and between two roots or tubers may be speared. Thrust the fork well down and under, then lift the root and throw it forward. Shake off the tubers and spread them out to dry, then fork through the place where the root has been in case any stragglers have been missed.

Leave the tubers on the soil for an hour or two to dry, then pick them up and rub the loose soil off them. The ware (eating) potatoes should be put into deep boxes or paper sacks. Plastic sacks are not suitable. Tubers too small for table use must also be picked up or they will turn up again as self-sets.

To keep through the winter months the tubers must be stored in a dark, cool and frost-proof place. Garden sheds are seldom frost-proof; if tubers have to be stored there, provide extra coverings during frosty spells. A few weeks after harvesting, take the tubers out into the light and sort them through again. Any tubers which may have been

Lifting potatoes; (*insert*) cross-section of clamp

carrying disease when they were lifted will have deteriorated still further, and can now be spotted and picked out.

If the crop exceeds several sacks it will be worth making a clamp in the garden. This provides ideal storage conditions and saves indoor space. The only materials needed are straw, hay, or dried bracken.

To make the clamp, tread the soil firm and then put down a layer of straw several inches thick. Pile the potatoes out on to the straw and build them up into a conical heap, making it as compact as possible. Now cover the heap with about 15cm (6in) of straw and then mark out a circle about 25cm (10in) from the straw. This is the ledge on which the soil will be built up.

Dig the soil out from beyond the circle and pack it up layer by layer on the cone, following the curve of the heap as it goes up. Cracks and hollows are filled in with loose soil from the bottom of the trench, which should be extended outwards, not downwards, as subsoil should not be used. Leave a tuft of straw sticking out at the top so that air can get into the heap. Later, when wintry conditions arrive, pull this out and fill in the hole.

When a supply of tubers has been taken out, make sure that the heap is adequately sealed up again. Do not attempt to open the clamp during frosty weather. By late March the tubers will have started to sprout. It is time then to break up the heap, rub off the sprouts, and take the tubers indoors.

Jerusalem Artichokes

Another vegetable which produces tubers is the Jerusalem artichoke. The tubers are smaller than those of the potato and have no starch content. As they are not affected by frost they can remain in the ground all winter.

Select tubers of even size and shape (an initial supply can be bought from seedsmen) and plant them 10cm (4in) deep in February or March, with 38cm (15in) between the tubers and 75cm (30in) between the rows. The stems reach a height of 2.5–3m (8–10ft) and need supporting with wires and stakes. Because of their height the plants make

Jerusalem artichoke

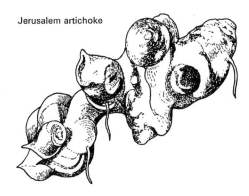

an excellent windbreak. When the foliage has been blackened by frost digging can begin. The tubers are not subject to virus diseases, and selected tubers from one's own crop can be used year after year.

Radishes

Summary Radishes

Summer Radishes

The summer radish matures more quickly than any other vegetable. In ideal conditions—warm, showery weather—the roots can be ready for pulling in three to four weeks. They like a fertile soil but not one freshly manured. As most of the growth is made in the top few inches of soil, it is a good plan to enrich this by forking in a little organic fertilizer, eg hoof and horn, or fishmeal.

If the soil is light and dries out quickly, fork in some well-moistened peat to make the soil more moisture retentive. In dry periods water the plants well so that there is no check to growth. The best radishes are always those that have been grown quickly.

There is never any need to reserve space for radishes as this is the ideal intercrop. Sow them between the rows of slower-growing crops such as peas or beans, on ground reserved for brassicas, or on any strip that will not be needed for a few weeks.

Summer radishes may be either of finger length or turnip-rooted. Where a frame or cloches are available, sowings can be made as early as February. Outdoor sowings should be made from late March or April, and then throughout the spring and summer. Sow little and often—it is easy to get too many radishes !

Most of the trouble encountered in growing radishes can be traced to two faults : sowing too deeply or too thickly. My own experience has convinced me that the best method of growing radishes is to sow them thinly

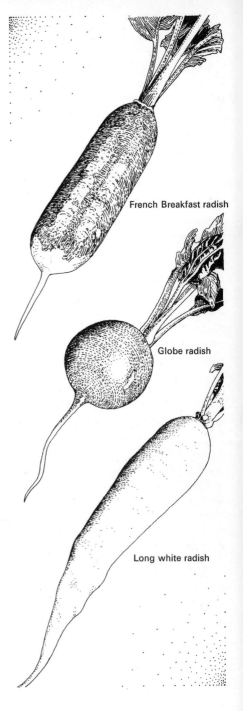

French Breakfast radish

Globe radish

Long white radish

on the soil surface in a band about 15cm (6in) wide. A good raking will put most of the seeds under the soil.

The only pest likely to be a nuisance is the flea-beetle, which eats holes in the young leaves. At the first sign of trouble dust the plants with derris or a proprietary flea-beetle dust.

Pull the roots as soon as they are large enough to eat. If they are left too long they become 'hot' and 'woody'. Take care when picking so that the other plants are disturbed as little as possible. Most sowings will give several pickings. After this, the residue is unlikely to be worth eating ; run the hoe through them, weeds and all.

Winter Radishes

Winter radishes are not as popular as summer ones, but are useful for winter salads. They make large roots which can be left in the ground all winter.

They are a good follow-on crop as they do not need to be sown until July or August. Sow the seeds in drills 25cm (10in) apart and thin the seedlings to stand 10–15cm (4–6in) apart. No special cultivation is required.

Recommended varieties

Summer radishes : French Breakfast, (long) red, with white tip ; Icicle (long), all white ; Sparkler and Cherry Belle (both turnip-rooted)
Winter radishes : China Rose, rose skin, white flesh ; Black Spanish, black skin with white flesh (roots may be either long or round)

Sowing radishes

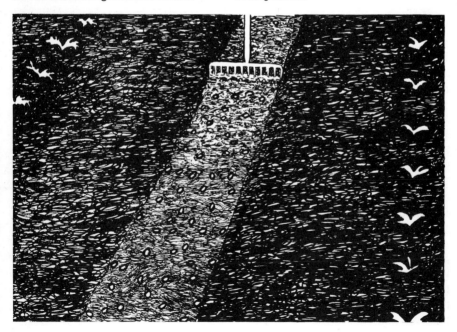

Rhubarb

If given good treatment, rhubarb will crop freely for many years. As the roots are perennial a permanent site must be found for them. For convenience of access, the most favoured situations are across one end of the plot or down a pathside, and there is no objection to this provided that the site is in full sun. Because the plants will be there for many years, the ground should be well prepared, and this is one occasion where double-digging will be of benefit. A strip 5.5 × 1.5m (18 × 5ft) will take six plants, which is ample for the average family.

To double-dig the chosen strip, take out a trench 60cm (24in) wide, shovel out the loose soil, then break up the subsoil with a fork. Put some manure or good compost in the trench, then fill it in with the topsoil taken out from the next strip. The last trench is filled in with the soil from the first one. As each lot of topsoil is put back, mix in some bonemeal at 140g per sq m (4oz per sq yd). Do this work some weeks before planting so that the soil has time to settle down.

The quickest way of obtaining rhubarb is to buy one-year-old roots and plant them in November, February or March. Dig a hole with the spade and plant each root so that the crowns (growing points) are about 5cm (2in) below the soil surface.

Do not pull any sticks the first season after planting, and pull only lightly during the second season. The leaves, as they die off in autumn, give their support to the crowns, and, by building up strong crowns, a more productive bed is assured. For the same reason no crown should ever be cropped too severely, and pulling should cease at the end of June. Stalks which form after then should be left to feed the crowns.

Rhubarb may also be grown from seeds which are sown in April in drills 2cm (1in) deep and 38cm (15in) apart. Thin the seedlings to stand 30cm (12in) apart. They will vary widely in quality, and it will be necessary to leave them for a second season in order to pick out the best and strongest roots. No stalks should be taken from these, but they may be pulled from the rejected plants.

To maintain the bed in good condition, rake off the dead leaves each autumn and then spread a layer of good compost over the bed.

Seed heads take the strength from the plants and should be cut out as they appear. If, after a long period, the stalks become weaker and thinner it will be a sign that the roots need lifting and dividing. Dig them out, select the best and youngest crowns for replanting (they will be on the outside) and throw the old roots away.

Mild forcing of the roots can be done by covering the whole bed with a 15cm (6in) layer of straw in January. Another method is to cover selected roots with old buckets or tubs so that light is excluded and a little extra warmth given, but do not choose the same roots each year.

Recommended varieties

Champagne Early, Victoria, Glaskin's Perpetual

49

Shallots and Garlic

Shallots

There is an old gardening tradition that shallots should be planted on the shortest day and harvested on the longest. This does not always work, but it does give an indication of how hardy the shallot is. It can, in fact, be planted from December to March.

The shallot is one of the easiest vegetables to grow. The type of soil is not important, but it should be healthy. A strip that was dug and manured in the autumn is ideal.

An initial supply of bulbs can be obtained from any good seedsman or garden centre. There are two types, red and yellow, and for most purposes there is little to choose between them. The yellow shallot is a little larger and is generally preferred for exhibition purposes. For future crops, simply pick out firm bulbs of medium size from the current crop.

Plant the bulbs in rows 30cm (12in) apart, with 20cm (8in) between the bulbs. The best method of planting is to make a small hole with the point of the trowel, and sit the bulb in the hole with about one-third of it showing above ground. Birds may cause a nuisance by pulling the bulbs out again, but this can easily be prevented by running some black cotton over them or covering them with pea guards. When the tips of the bulbs show green they will have rooted and there should be no further trouble.

Although the bulbs are not damaged by frost, it will sometimes lift them a little; if this happens firm them in again. Keep them clean, but do not hoe too close to them or too deeply around them. Each bulb will split up to form a cluster of new bulbs.

By the end of June or in July,

Shallot bulbs planted in rows

according to the seasonal weather, the tops will turn yellow and flop over. The bulbs can then be lifted. To harvest them ease them with a fork, then pull them out and leave them on the ground to dry. Do not split them up at this stage. In warm, dry weather they can be dried off without difficulty ; in cool, showery weather the roots may take hold of the soil again. To prevent this, remove them to a hard surface or put a few cloches over them. When the bulbs are quite dry and the tops withered, break up the clusters and rub off any loose skin.

Store the bulbs by spreading them out thinly in a light, cool and frost-proof place. The best method is to ask your greengrocer for a few shallow tomato trays and store the bulbs in these.

Garlic

Garlic is not difficult to grow. It likes a light to medium loam in good heart, and in full sun. A garlic bulb, as every garlic user knows, is made up of a number of segments or cloves. If these are planted in February, 5cm (2in) deep, with 20cm (8in) between the cloves and 30cm (12in) between the rows, they will grow on to form bulbs. No special cultivation is required. If flower heads form, pinch them out.

About the end of July the foliage turns yellow, and this is the sign to lift the bulbs. The harvesting and storing process is the same as for shallots.

Recommended varieties

Shallots : Giant Red, Giant Yellow
Garlic : Italian ; the easiest method is to buy a bulb from the shop in the ordinary way and use this.

Easing shallot bulbs

Garlic and shallot

Spinach and Spinach Beet

Spinach beet

Spinach between
rows of peas

Spinach

Spinach is known to the housewife as a plant rich in iron, and to the gardener as the vegetable which holds the record for bolting ! Summer spinach is easy to grow, but it does like a soil well supplied with humus which will retain moisture. On light, hungry soils the bolting tendency is increased.

The plants are usually grown as an intercrop between rows of slower-growing vegetables such as peas or beans. The seeds of summer spinach are round, and it is sometimes referred to as round-seeded spinach. Sow the seeds from March to June in drills 13mm ($\frac{1}{2}$in) deep. As the period of harvesting is relatively short sowings every two or three weeks are needed to keep up a supply.

When the plants are large enough to handle, thin them to stand 8cm (3in) apart, and then take out every other plant when it is large enough to use. Mature plants can be picked over several times by taking the largest leaves first. Cut, or pinch them off, close up to the stem.

Dryness at the roots is another reason why the plants go to seed, so make sure they never lack water. Plants maturing during July or August will welcome the shade given by taller crops.

Winter spinach is also known as Prickly Spinach. This description is applied to the seeds, not the plants. It is hardier than the summer type and does not go to seed as quickly.

A strip of ground that was well manured for a previous crop is the best choice. As the seeds are not sown until August or September it is customary to use this as a follow-on crop to earlier vegetables. Sowings made at this time will give pickings from November until early April. Sow the seeds in rows 13mm ($\frac{1}{2}$in) deep and 30cm (12in) apart, and thin to 20cm (8in) apart. In February a little nitro-chalk at about 35g per metre run (1oz per yard run) will help to boost production.

Take only the largest leaves from each plant and do not take too many from one plant at a time as growth is slower during the winter months. The plants are hardy, but a better and cleaner crop will be otained if they are covered with cloches early in October.

Spinach Beet

This plant, which is also known as Perpetual Spinach, is an excellent spinach substitute. The leaves are larger and fleshier than those of the true spinach and the plants, being biennial, do not go to seed until their second year. Each plant forms a root like a beetroot, but it is grown for the leaves, not the root. When the larger leaves are removed, others grow to replace them.

Sow the seeds in drills 13mm ($\frac{1}{2}$in) deep and 38cm (15in) apart, and thin the plants to 20cm (8in) apart. A sowing can be made in April for summer use, and another in July or August for use in spring and early summer.

Recommended varieties

Summer Spinach : Viking, Long-
  standing Round
Winter Spinach : Greenmarket, Long-
  standing Prickly
Spinach Beet : usually listed as Spinach
  Beet or Perpetual Spinach

Sweet Corn

The plants do best in a medium loam, well supplied with humus. Heavy soils are not as suitable as they take too long to warm up. If manure or compost cannot be spared, choose a site that was well manured for the previous crop, and supplement this with a general fertilizer at 70g per sq m (2oz per sq yd), applied when the soil is worked down.

There are several ways of starting off the plants. If a cold greenhouse or frame is available, they can be raised in 9cm (3½in) pots, two seeds being sown in a pot. If both grow, pull one out. Sweet corn is only half-hardy and cannot be planted out while there is a risk of frost.

Another method, suitable for the cloche owner, is to sow two rows 38cm (15in) apart under barn cloches in April, and keep the plants covered until June. For an outdoor sowing without protection, sow the seeds about the middle of May, 5cm (2in) deep, with 30cm (12in) between the plants and 38cm (15in) between the rows.

The plants do not like root disturbance and if transplanting has to be done it should be done as carefully as possible. Peat or cardboard pots which break up after planting are often used for sweet corn.

Hoe carefully, as the plants are not deep rooting, and water well if the weather is dry. Moisture can be conserved after watering if a mulch of peat or lawn mowings is put down between the rows. In July and August the plants will respond well to foliar

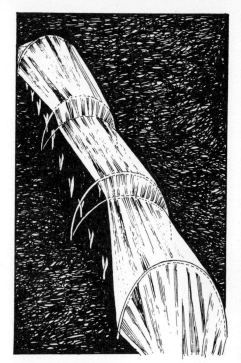

Sweet corn under cloche

feeding.

It helps to anchor the plants if a little soil is drawn up around the base of the stems. As they are subject to wind damage some kind of staking is advisable. One method is to use stout bamboo canes for each row, and run garden wire between them. Individual plants can then be tied to the wires.

The plants are decorative, and unusual, in that each plant carries both male and female parts. Fertilization takes place when the pollen from the male 'tassels' at the top of the plant is caught by the female 'silks' at the end of each immature cob. Each silk is a tuft of fine, silky hairs which turn brown as the cob ripens. Planting a number of short rows to form a block will make fertilization more effective

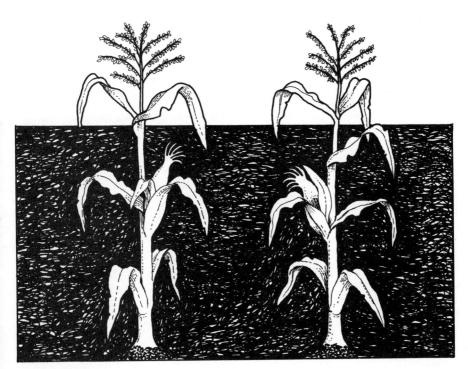

Sweet corn plants

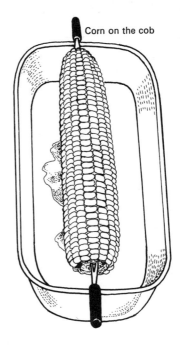

Corn on the cob

and will also make staking easier.

Part of the art of growing sweet corn lies in knowing when the cobs are ready for gathering. The browning and withering of the silks is one guide. The most reliable way of judging the correct moment for harvesting is to turn back a little of the sheath until the grains are visible and then pierce a grain with a thumb-nail. If the liquid that comes out is watery, leave the cob a little longer; the ideal stage for eating is when the liquid is milky. Detach the cob with a quick twist and cook as soon as possible after gathering.

Recommended varieties

John Innes Hybrid (F1 hybrid),
   Earliking (F1 hybrid), Golden
   Bantam

Outdoor Tomatoes

To some extent, success with outdoor tomatoes must always be dependent on weather conditions, but the introduction of new varieties and the bush tomato, coupled with the use of cloches, have made it less of a gamble than it used to be.

A medium loam in good heart suits them well enough, but the type of soil is actually of less importance than the site, which should be a sunny one, preferably with some shelter from cold winds. A south-facing wall or boarded fence is ideal, as heat will be reflected back on to the plants.

Plants may be bought in, if desired, but the choice of varieties is limited. Choose plants which are short jointed and of a good, deep colour. The plants can be raised without much trouble if a cool greenhouse is available. Sow the seeds in a seed-pan early in April, and prick them off into 9cm (3½in) pots when the first true leaves have formed. Keep them well to the light and harden them off thoroughly before planting out. Gardeners without a greenhouse can raise enough plants for a family by starting them off in the sunny window of a warm room. Turn the pots daily to keep the plants from growing to one side.

Unless the plants can be put out under frames or cloches, transplanting cannot take place until the risk of frost has passed. In most districts this will be early June. Put them out 45cm (18in) apart, with the soil ball covered by about 13mm (½in) of new soil.

It helps the plants to get off to a good start if they can be given some protection from cold winds for the first few weeks after planting. Strips of plastic joined together or plastic bags cut open and secured to bamboo canes, make an effective screen.

Outdoor tomatoes are of two types— cordon and bush—but it should be remembered that any tomato plant, if left to its own devices, will make a bush. Growing the plants as cordons (ie keeping them to one main stem) is done to produce better and earlier fruits. The side-shoots, which form in the axils of the leaves, should be pinched out as they appear. When each plant has set four or five trusses (branches) of fruit, pinch out the growing point.

Bush plants under barn cloche

Bush tomatoes, on the other hand, do not need any training except perhaps to cut out superfluous shoots. They are excellent for growing under barn cloches.

Cordon varieties can be fed with a proprietary tomato fertilizer once the bottom fruits have set. Bush tomatoes do not need feeding; on too rich a diet they tend to produce foliage at the expense of fruit.

Covering the plants with frames or cloches, if only for a few weeks until they grow too big, is of great benefit, and similar protection at the end of the season will assist ripening. Cordon varieties should be cut from their stakes in September and laid on clean straw or black plastic. Bush plants, pulled down with fruit, can have cloches put over them. Ripening will then continue into October. After that, pick all the fruit and take it indoors. Many will still ripen if they are kept in a basket in a warm living-room or kitchen. Cover them with a cloth.

Outdoor tomatoes are not subject to as many pests and diseases as their indoor cousins. Slugs may be troublesome, especially with the bush varieties. Potato blight can be deadly and spraying should be done, as for potatoes.

Recommended varieties

Outdoor cordons : Outdoor Girl, Marmande
Bush tomatoes : French Cross (F1 hybrid) and Sleaford Abundance (F1 hybrid) are two varieties that give heavy crops of good-quality fruit

Pinching out side-shoots

Turnips, Swedes and Kohl Rabi

Turnips

Turnip varieties can be divided into two groups : the early summer ones, and the later ones which can be stored for winter use.

The summer varieties need a soil with a good humus content which will not dry out too quickly. Medium to heavy loams usually fill this need. On light soils these turnips can prove difficult, especially in a hot summer.

Sow the summer varieties from March to June in drills 13mm ($\frac{1}{2}$in) deep and 30cm (12in) apart, and thin the seedlings to stand 10–15cm (4–6in) apart. It is better to make several small sowings than one large one ; the roots can then be used before they become too big.

Turnips for winter storage should be sown towards the end of June or in July. These should stand 15cm (6in) apart and will crop from October onwards. They can be used as a follow-on vegetable. To prepare a bed for them apply a dressing of a general fertilizer at 70g per sq m (2oz per sq yd) and prick it into the top few inches of soil.

In November the turnips can be lifted for storage. Cut off the tops an inch or two from the crown, trim the roots a little, and then store the turnips in boxes of dry sand or soil.

Swede

Milan White

Swedes

Swedes may be sown in May or June. They need similar conditions to turnips. Sow them thinly in drills 38cm (15in) apart and thin out to 20cm (8in). They are hardier than turnips and can stay out all winter. The garden swede is a little smaller than the field swede.

In the spring any swedes which are left will make new tops. These are rich in iron and can be cut for use as a vegetable. Where they are appreciated a sowing can be made especially for this purpose. This sowing need not be made until August and need not be thinned.

Kohl Rabi

Where turnips prove difficult it is often recommended that kohl rabi should be grown instead. This is good advice as this vegetable is less demanding in its soil requirements and will grow in any good garden soil. But it is also well worth growing as a vegetable in its own right. It has a nutty, turnip-like flavour and its popularity is increasing. The plant is rather curious in that it forms the edible root above the ground. The root is, in fact, the swollen stem of the plant which bulges out like a ball. It is at its best when it is between golf- and cricket-ball size.

Kohl rabi may be sown from March to early August in shallow drills 38cm (15in) apart. Thin the plants to stand 15cm (6in) apart. There is a white form and a purple form of this vegetable.

Being brassicas, turnips, swedes and kohl rabi can all be attacked by club root (see Brassicas—General). It is wise, therefore, to keep them clear of badly-infected soil and change their site each year. The flea-beetle may

Kohl rabi

plague them when they have just broken through the soil, but this can be dealt with by dusting the seedlings with derris or a flea-beetle dust.

Recommended varieties

Summer turnips : Milan White, Snowball

Winter turnips : Manchester Market, Golden Ball

Swedes : Purple Top

Kohl rabi : White Vienna, Earliest Purple

Vegetable Marrows, Courgettes and Pumpkins

Marrows and Courgettes

Nowadays the large marrow is out of favour and the trend is for smaller fruits. Courgettes, now so popular, are simply baby marrows cut when they are very small.

The vegetable marrow can be grown in most soils. Light soils will need enriching with manure or compost to help them retain moisture. Heavy soils should be opened up with strawy manure or rough compost to improve the drainage and to prevent water from gathering round the roots of the plants.

Plants can be raised by making a sowing in pots in a frame or cool greenhouse in April. Push two seeds down on edge in a 9cm (3½in) pot and pull the weaker seedling out if both germinate. Marrows are only half-hardy and cannot be planted out until the risk of frost has passed. They do not like root disturbance and should be moved with care. Peat or cardboard pots, which break up after planting, should be used for them. The object of this method is to gain a few weeks of growing time.

An easier method is to push in the seeds where the plants are to grow. This can be done during the middle of May, planting three seeds in a triangle, 10cm (4in) apart, then selecting the best plant for growing on ; allow 122cm (48in) between the plants.

Marrows and courgettes

Beyond seeing that the plants are kept clean, and that they do not lack water during dry periods, no special care is needed. Fertilization should occur naturally with outdoor plants, but if the flowers fall off without setting, hand fertilization can be done by stripping a male flower of its petals and pushing it into the heart of a female flower. The females are easy to recognize as they have an embryo marrow behind the flower.

Some varieties produce long vines (trailing shoots) on which the fruits form. The bush varieties grow in a circle. It is not always realized that the trailing varieties will climb. This makes them suitable for planting at the foot of a fence or trellis. Some of the vines may need to be tied up, and hanging fruits should be supported or their weight may pull the vines down again.

Cut the fruits when they are large enough to use and others will follow. For use as courgettes the fruits need not be more than 10–15cm (4–6in) long. Some varieties are better than others for producing courgettes, but their cultivation is exactly the same as for ordinary marrows.

Pumpkin

Recommended varieties

Marrows : Long White Trailing ; White Bush ; Long Green Trailing ; Green Bush ; Table Dainty, a trailing green marrow of medium size

Courgettes : Zucchine (F1 hybrid), green bush ; Golden Zucchine (F1 hybrid), yellow bush

Pumpkins : Hundredweight, the standard variety

Pumpkins

Pumpkins are grown in the same way as marrows, but need to be 2m (6ft) apart. The fruits of pumpkins should be left to ripen and then cut around the end of September. Limit each plant to two or three fruits so that they reach a good size.

Surplus marrows may also be left to ripen on the plants. If the ripe fruits of pumpkins and marrows are stored in a dry, warm place they will keep sound for several months.

Basic Herbs

Because they are found so often in vegetable gardens or on allotments, there are five herbs that can fairly be described as basic herbs. They all do well in a good, medium loam and a sunny position, and will succeed also in heavier soils provided that drainage is good. They are chives, parsley, sage, thyme and mint.

Chives

This plant resembles spring onions both in appearance and in flavour. It sends up a profusion of slender leaves which can be cut off about 5cm (2in) above soil level. New shoots soon appear. The foliage dies down in winter and reappears in spring. If the clumps are not cut attractive blue flowers are formed. An initial supply can be obtained by growing seeds in April. Thereafter, it is only necessary to divide the clumps as needed in autumn or spring.

Parsley

The best time for sowing parsley is in February and March, and again in July. Parsley is a biennial and goes to seed in its second year. Germination is very slow (it is said that parsley goes nine times to the devil before coming up !) and it is a good plan to sow a few radish seeds with the parsley so that the row can be picked out for weeding. Thin the plants to stand 25–30cm (10–12in) apart. This gives finer plants and better leaves. If the plants are covered with a cloche or two in the autumn, fresh parsley can be picked all through the winter. Some people are

Parsley

convinced that pouring boiling water on the newly-seeded bed makes the plants come up faster.

Sage

The best sage for most purposes is the broad-leaved sage. This is a shrubby, perennial plant about 45cm (18in) high, with grey-green leaves. Cuttings of broad-leaved sage root readily, if planted in May. After a few years the plants tend to get leggy and should be replaced with rooted cuttings. The narrow-leaved sage bears a purple flower and can be grown from seed.

Thyme

A good thyme bush will be about 30cm (12in) high and as much as 90cm (36in) across. The common thyme is the most popular. It can be grown from seeds, sown in the spring. The other method of propagation is to draw soil up all around a plant and peg the thyme into the soil. New roots soon form. The plant has a delightful fragrance when the leaves are bruised and is quite hardy.

Mint

There are several forms of mint, but spearmint is the most common. Mint in an invasive plant which grows by thrusting out its roots into the surrounding soil. New shoots are sent up from the joints of the roots. Start off with a few roots and plant them in early spring about 5cm (2in) deep. The easiest method of planting is to take out a shallow trench with the spade, spread the roots out along the trench and then cover them. Mint tends to grow outwards, leaving the middle of the bed bare, and as it has to be hand-weeded it is a good plan to make a fresh bed every few years. Some people keep it within bounds by growing it in an old bucket or tin bath sunk into the soil. It will grow in partial shade.

Mint is subject to a fungus disease called rust which produces brown spots underneath the leaves. The best cure is to burn the foliage off in the autumn by forking dry straw or litter among the stems so that the flames sweep through quickly.

Thyme

Mint

Further reading from David & Charles

GOOD FOOD GROWING GUIDE
Gardening and Living Nature's Way
John Bond and the Staff of 'Mother Earth'
A new-look growing guide to healthier and happier living
241 × 148mm   illustrated

ECONOMY COOK BOOK
Mary Griffiths
A guide to how to cope with rising food and housekeeping prices and still produce tasty and nutritious meals
216 × 138mm

COST-EFFECTIVE SELF-SUFFICIENCY
or The Middle-Class Peasant
Eve and Terence McLaughlin
A practical guide to self-sufficiency, proving that life as 'middle-class peasants' is not only viable but enormously enjoyable and satisfying
247 × 171mm   illustrated

EAT CHEAPLY AND WELL
Brenda Sanctuary
Rising food prices make this up-to-the-minute book a must for today's housewives
216 × 138mm   illustrated

GROWPLAN VEGETABLE BOOK
A Month-by-Month Guide
Peter Peskett and Geoff Amos
A practical, easy-reference guide to growing super vegetables, and fruit too, month by month
250 × 200mm   illustrated

GROWING FOOD UNDER GLASS:
1001 Questions Answered
Adrienne and Peter Oldale
An indispensable guide to setting up and maintaining every kind of glasshouse, together with an A–Z rundown of the familiar and unusual fruit and vegetables to be grown
210 × 148mm   illustrated

GROWING FRUIT:
1001 Questions Answered
Adrienne and Peter Oldale
Answers all the questions a novice might ask about pests and diseases, choice of tree shapes and varieties, and pruning techniques
210 × 148mm   illustrated

GROWING VEGETABLES:
1001 Questioned Answered
Adrienne and Peter Oldale
All you need to know about growing vegetables in a simple question and answer format
210 × 148mm   illustrated

COMPLETE BOOK OF HERBS AND SPICES
Claire Loewenfeld and Philippa Back
A comprehensive guide to every aspect of herbs and spices—their history and traditions. cultivation, uses in the kitchen, and health and cosmetics
242 × 184mm   illustrated

COOK OUT
Frances Kitchin
For the cook on a caravanning or camping holiday, Frances Kitchin provides the answers to all the problems when cooking meals with the minimum of facilities
210 × 132mm   illustrated

British Library Cataloguing in Publication Data

Hall, Martyn T.
    Easy vegetable growing.—(Penny pinchers).
    1. Vegetable gardening
    I. Title   II. Rn: Morris, David, b.1912 (Mar.)
    III. Series
    635   SB322

    ISBN 0–7153–7547–4

First published 1978
Second impression 1979

© David & Charles Ltd 1978

Set in Univers
and printed in Great Britain
by Redwood Burn Limited
for David & Charles (Publishers) Limited
Brunel House   Newton Abbot   Devon

Published in the United States of America
by David & Charles Inc
North Pomfret   Vermont 05053   USA